Shot!

Compiled by Doug Cheeseman, Mike Alway and Andy Lyons

Shot!

A Photographic Record of
Football in the Seventies

Foreword by **Eamonn McCabe**

H. F. & G. Witherby

Published in association with
When Saturday Comes

Foreword

By Eamonn McCabe

It was Gary Glitter's fault I started photographing football in the first place. Like a lot of teenage blokes I was music daft, but I was also tone deaf, so the nearest I could get to a stage was to photograph the bands I worshipped. I got myself a job printing for a rock and roll photographer and for a few years in the early seventies I was in my element. The great thing about photographing bands like The Who and The Stones was that no matter how many times you covered them you never knew what you were going to get, that was the thrill. Then along came Gary. After the third time I photographed the 'Leader of the Gang', I was bored. It was always the same. His shirt would mysteriously burst open at the same spot on the stage every time. I wanted more. In the darkroom next to mine they printed sports pictures. I was so bored with Glitter and co, I offered my services to the sports agency next door and one Saturday they gave me the job of photographing Tottenham versus Southampton. I got reasonable pictures of Martin Chivers, 'the

complete centre forward', scoring and two Sunday papers used them.

A few months later I got some freelance work with the *Guardian* working alongside Frank Keating. One Saturday we went to Chelmsford to photograph the comeback from retirement of my all-time hero, Jimmy Greaves. His comeback lasted a matter of minutes, his back went and I had hardly got a picture. We decided to follow him into the dressing room. There he was in the shower. Great picture, I thought, real behind the scenes stuff. I lifted my camera to my eye and he went for me, 'If you take a picture of me with that, I'll shove it up your arse.' But, Jim, it's me, I wanted to tell him, I used to get to the front of the terrace hours before kick-off just to see you and Gillie . . . But I couldn't spit the words out and had to make do with some shots of talking heads in the bar afterwards. Boring.

That phrase, 'I'll shove it up your arse', must be something footballers are taught in training. I heard it again, from Mick Kennedy of Bradford, when I spent a

year with them in 1988. He was smoking a pipe at the time and obviously thought it was too passive an image for such a well-known hard man, but I got the picture that time.

The two worst moments I remember from the seventies were both painful and embarrassing. The first was at Arsenal. I was photographing the kick-in before a game with Wolves. Willie Carr was shooting into the net at the Clock End and I was getting some good stock pictures when suddenly a ball came straight at my head. I ducked and brought up my camera at the same time, knocking half my front tooth out. There was blood everywhere and the game was just starting. The messenger from the *Observer* was waiting to go back to the office with the film from the first few minutes. Needless to say I did not have very much.

The other was also at an Arsenal match, this time in Amsterdam against Ajax. I got caught at the wrong end at the kick-off (my sports editor thought Arsenal might score for some strange reason) and

decided to run straight from goalpost to goalpost with all my gear. I got to the halfway line with 40,000 fans cheering me on when I tripped over my camera strap and fell right on the centre spot. It was the great Johan Cruyff who picked me up. The walk to the other end was the longest I can remember.

Photographing football in the seventies was a joy. Agents hadn't even been thought about. The players were far more available, they even seemed to enjoy the skills of others. You could go training on a Friday and photograph the latest signing or groin strain without asking anybody's permission. The clubs loved it, it helped fill the grounds. As the pictures in this book show, the players posed for, rather than played up to, the camera. The portraits of Malcolm Allison and George Graham are noble; even the *Playboy*-like pose of Gary Sprake somehow seems right. The great crowd shots make you wish you'd been there. As photographers, we were invited to photograph the managers and the players behind the scenes,

in the corridors; that's what the fans wanted to see.

The best thing about working in the seventies was that there were no adverts. We could work on any side of the ground. But with these huge boards aimed at the TV lens, it's hard to get a clean background. And now that TV is God, the clubs don't care about papers any more. In these money-grabbing times it is easier to cover the Bosnian war than Arsenal training. But maybe I was lucky. I'd far rather photograph Alfie Conn than Gascoigne any time. After all, as I learned from my association with Gary Glitter, it is not very hard to photograph a man with his tongue sticking out.

Eamonn McCabe was Sports Photographer of the Year in 1978, 1979, 1981 and 1984. He is now Picture Editor of the *Guardian*.

Body Language
Ray Clemence
stretches out at
Melwood, Liverpool's
training ground

Circa 1975

Throw Back
Chelsea's Ian
Hutchinson hones his
secret weapon

20th January 1972

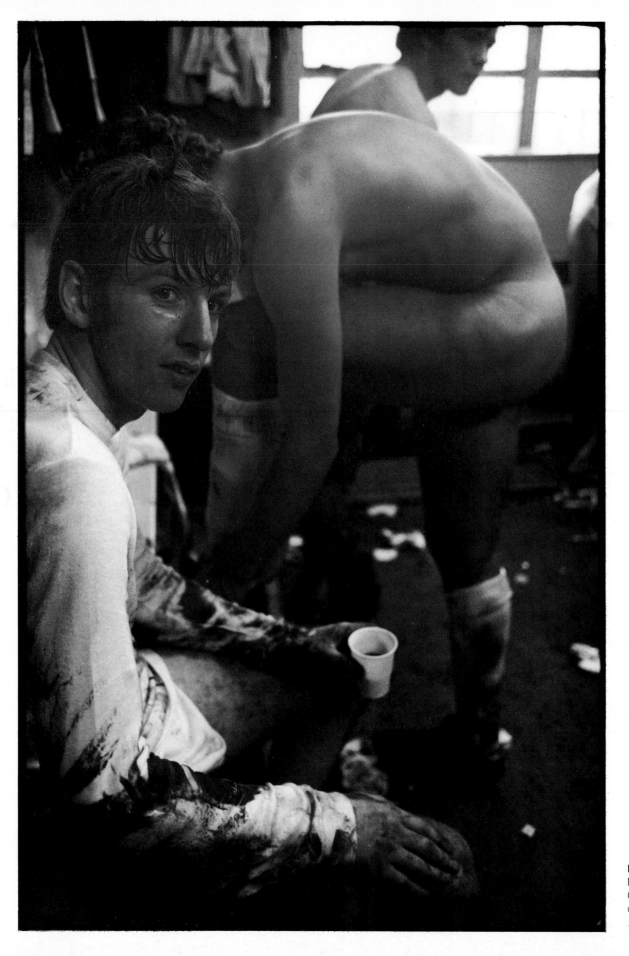

Dressing Down
Martin Peters and Martin
Chivers unwind in the Spurs
changing room

1971–72

11 of 120

Fair Exchange
Ze Maria has been booked after repeatedly
fouling Peter Barnes, but they still shake
hands at the end of England's 1–1 draw
with Brazil at Wembley

19th April 1978

Goal Bound
Geoff Hurst scores for
Stoke City

22nd March 1975

Matter Of Opinion
Johan Cruyff is sent off by Señor J Orrianda
during Barcelona's 3–2 defeat at Malaga in
a Spanish League match

9th February 1975

Easily Dismissed
Billy Bremner, sent off along with
Kevin Keegan. The Charity Shield
would never be this interesting again

Leeds v Liverpool
10th August 1974

Local Hero
Newcastle centre forward
Malcolm MacDonald bent
double under the weight of
his sideburns

1971

Fever Pitch
Ronnie Radford has scored the equalizer for
non-League Hereford United against First
Division Newcastle United, in an FA Cup 3rd
Round replay; the pitch is awash with snorkel
parkas. Hereford won in extra time

6th February 1972

Sign Of The Times
Stan Bowles and Don Givens of Queen's Park Rangers swap congratulations

25th September 1976

Moment In Time
Colin Stein scores a last-minute equalizer against
Celtic. Rangers fans leaving in the belief that the game
was lost rushed back upon hearing the roar of the
crowd. Sixty-six people died in the resulting crush

Ibrox
2nd January 1971

Best Remembered
George in training

1972

Told In Confidence

'I don't accept that you do a good job in football without upsetting somebody along the way.'
Brighton manager and ITV panelist Brian Clough

25th January 1974

Pitch Inspectors
Bill Shankly and Bill Nicholson endeavour to keep the White Hart Lane mud off their match-day suits

Circa 1974

Football Focus
Tottenham players watch a television
preview of their forthcoming game
against Wolves on the opening day
of the 1971–72 season

14th August 1971

Pastures New
Ossie Ardiles relaxing
on his first day at Spurs

July 1978

Bob And Frank
Wilson and Worthington in action,
League Division One, Huddersfield 2
Arsenal 1. Arsenal went on to win the
double; two seasons later Huddersfield
were relegated to Division Three

16th January 1971

Spanish Eyes
Two and a half years after leaving Orient, Laurie
Cunningham is about to play for Real Madrid
against Barcelona. He scored in a 3–2 home win

23rd September 1979

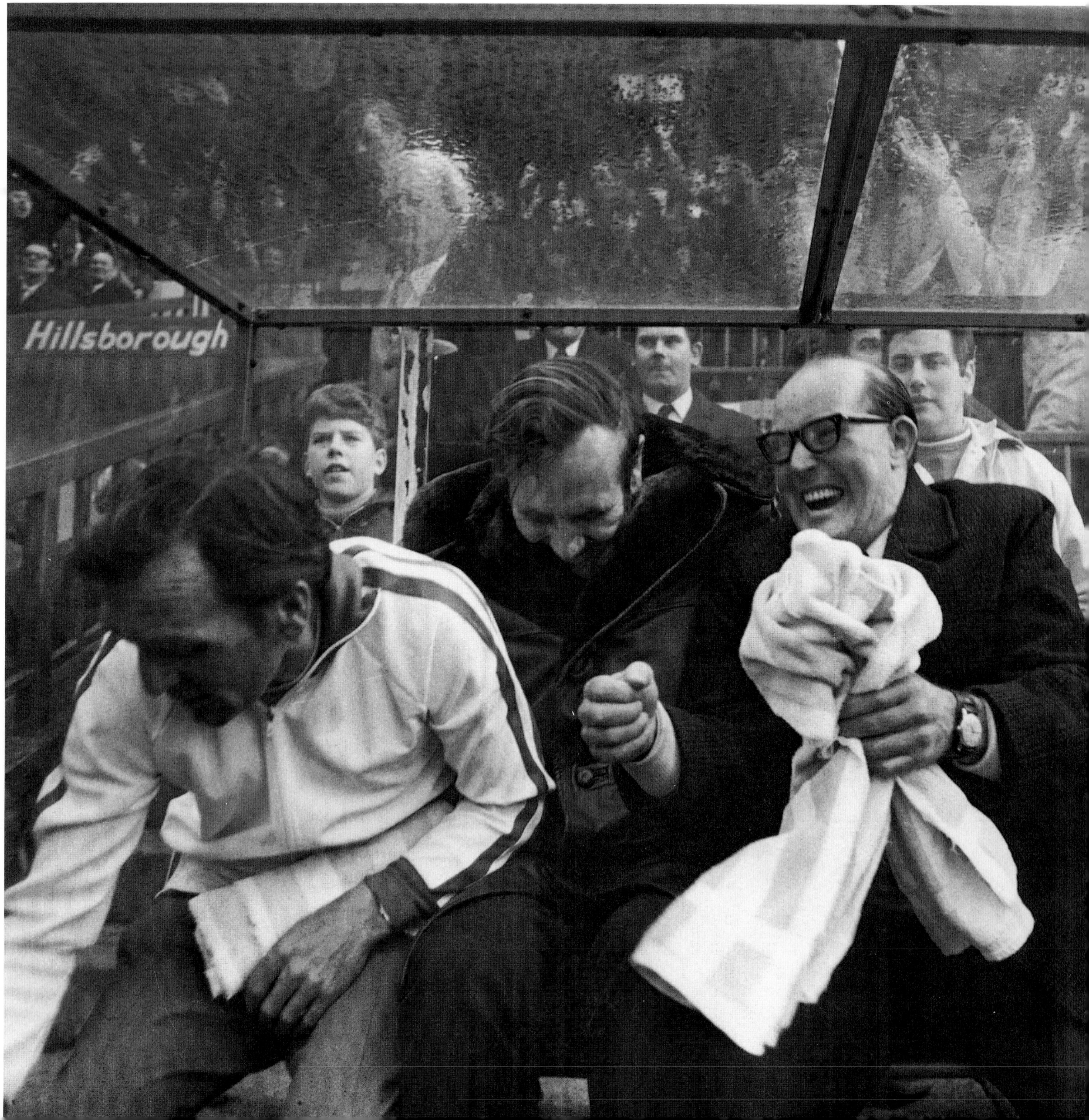
Hillsborough

Up For The Cup
The Leeds bench celebrate
one of their three goals during
their 3–0 FA Cup Semi-Final
win over Birmingham City

15th April 1972

Down Beat
Don Revie leaves Molineux after Leeds lose their last League
game of the 1972 season to Wolves. A win would have brought
them the double. In 1977 Leeds were accused by the *Daily Mirror*
of offering Wolves players a bribe to lose the match. Revie and
skipper Billy Bremner won the resulting libel case

8th May 1972

Detroit Spinner
While the rest of the world prepares
to go to Argentina, England's Trevor
Francis gets to grips with astroturf
prior to his NASL debut for Detroit
Express against Memphis Rogues

May 1978

Blues Brothers
Trevor Francis, Roger Hynd
and Bob Latchford run out to
expectant faces at St
Andrews, Birmingham

1973

Frozen In Time
Most of the FA Cup 3rd
Round ties are called off due
to the winter weather, but an
unscheduled game takes
place in Shoreditch. From left
to right: Roy Spencer, Danny
Brookes and Paul Day

6th January 1975

Seconds Out
The first of two penalties awarded during the
Holland v West Germany World Cup Final by the
English referee, Jack Taylor. Johan Neeskens is
about to put the Dutch ahead in the first minute,
before their opponents had even touched the ball.
The Germans came back to win 2–1

7th July 1974

Forward Thinking
Clyde Best, West Ham's
Bermudan striker

1971

Cardboard City
Polish international Kazimierz Deyna
sightseeing during the binmen's strike three
months after signing for Manchester City

22nd February 1979

Street Level

The pre-match scene outside
Brisbane Road before an
Orient home match

Circa 1974

Built For Speed
Bob Wilson relaxes in the summer
after Arsenal's double

July 1971

Stretcher Case
Arsenal goalkeeper Jimmy
Rimmer lies injured in his goal

17th April 1976

Previous page

Over And Out
2–1 down to Rochdale in the FA
Cup 3rd Round, Coventry squander
a late chance to equalize

11th January 1971

Centre Of Attention
England meet Denmark in a
European Championship qualifier

9th September 1979

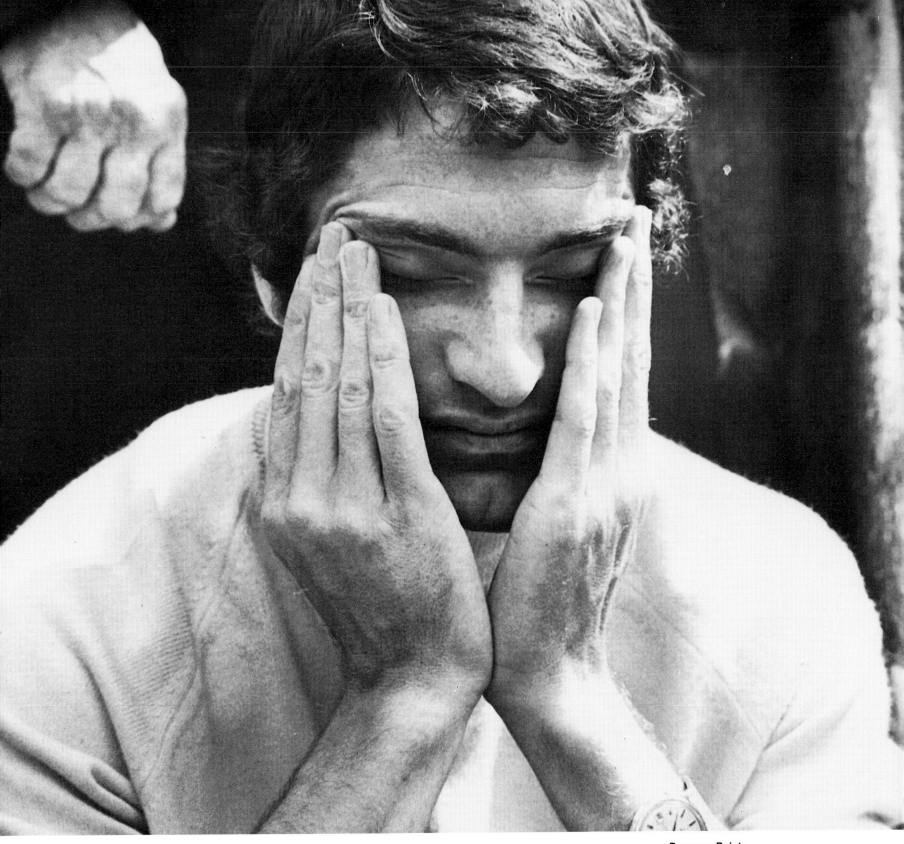

Pressure Points
The 1971 Footballer of the Year, Frank McLintock, braces himself before stepping out to be greeted by a 500,000 crowd assembled to salute the Arsenal double-winners at Islington Town Hall

10th May 1971

World In Motion
Johan Neeskens evades Brazilian
defender Luis Pereira to score in the
World Cup in Germany. Holland's
2–0 win took them to the Final

3rd July 1974

Blurred Memory
Archie Gemmill takes flight for
Nottingham Forest against
Grasshoppers of Zurich, in a
European Cup Quarter-Final

7th March 1979

Keeping Up Appearances
Peter Shilton ready to pull
out all the stops for
Leicester City at Arsenal

25th September 1971

Penalty Appeal
Jeff Astle adopts a direct approach to the
art of the spot-kick, but his team, West
Bromwich Albion, still lose the Watney
Cup Final shoot-out to Colchester

9th August 1971

A European Place
Kevin Keegan scores from the penalty spot as Liverpool beat Borussia Mönchengladbach 3–0 in the UEFA Cup Final, First Leg. Liverpool took the trophy 3–2 on aggregate

10th May 1973

Oblivious
The Tottenham tea-ladies leave
early to avoid the rush
Tottenham v Manchester United

4th March 1972

Mirror Image
Manchester United fans at Craven Cottage before a Division Two match against Fulham

26th October 1974

Smoke Signals
Cesar Luis Menotti
affecting disinterest in
the outcome of the
charity match between
his World All Stars XI
and the New York
Cosmos

30th August 1978

Office Politics
Franz Beckenbauer
talks shop

Circa 1973

Striking A Pose
A pristine Martin Chivers puts in
some extra shooting practice

Circa 1973

After Hours
Ted McDougall, Bournemouth's prolific
goalscorer, practises his finishing

Circa 1972

Gimme Shelter
Stadium security guards drag
away an AS Roma fan. Stoke City
had just beaten the home side 1–0
in the Anglo-Italian Cup

1st June 1971

Tunnel Vision
Santos' number 10
emerges into the light

Circa 1972

Previous page

Safe Keeping
Gary Sprake, Leeds
United goalkeeper

1970

The Getaway Vehicle
Dave Mackay leaves the Baseball
Ground after being sacked as
manager of Derby County

25th November 1976

Derby Winner
Kevin Hector and John
McGovern celebrate one of the
two goals that beat Spartak
Trnava of Czechoslovakia 2–1
on aggregate in a European
Cup Quarter-Final tie

21st March 1973

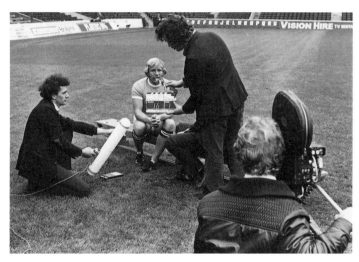

Screen Test
Francis Lee of Manchester City,
about to be interviewed for ITV's
Saturday lunchtime football preview,
On the Ball. Slate 16, take 1

Circa 1973

Attention Seeker
Johan Cruyff re-enters the field
after receiving treatment, while
playing for Holland against
Bulgaria in the World Cup Finals

23rd June 1974

Stretching The Point
Ray Wilkins of Chelsea catches
Burnley's Brian Flynn unawares
during a Division Two game

27th November 1976

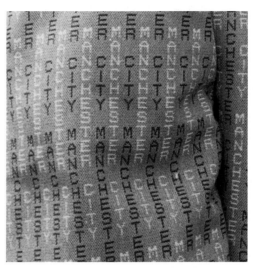

Suit Yourself
A jacket with Manchester City woven
through it, available from the supporters
club, with cardigan and tie, for £30.
Modelled by Ron Ashworth, who said,
'I think it is smashing - a great
advertisement for the club.'

1973

Cold Remedy
Leicester City's hot air balloon that covered
the Filbert Street pitch, allowing the team to
train at the ground throughout the winter

1972

Mud Lark
Ron Davies passes in
the mud for Wales
against Scotland

15th May 1971

Swapping Sides
England players after the
Home International fixture
with Scotland. Allan Clarke is
wearing Jim Holton's shirt

19th May 1973

Blood Sport
Joe Jordan bears the scars of
Leeds' European Cup Semi-Final
victory against Barcelona

24th March 1975

Men At Work
Tottenham players limber up

1971–72

In The Balance

Geoff Nulty of Burnley

1970

Billy Idol
Billy Bonds and a teenage lookalike
after West Ham have taken the lead
against Orient in a Texaco Cup tie

3rd August 1974

Final Straw
Barry Endean scores the winning
goal for Watford against Liverpool in
an FA Cup Quarter-Final. Watford
lost 5–1 to Chelsea in the Semis

21st February 1970

High Numbers
Roberto Boninsegna, ecstatic as he sets
Italy on their way to a 4–3 extra-time victory
over West Germany in the World Cup
Semi-Final. Brazil won 4–1 in the Final

17th June 1970

Trend Setter
Manchester City's assistant
manager and coach,
Malcolm Allison, models
early-period Adidas

August 1970

Chelsea Girls
All Chelsea have to do
now is beat Leeds in the
FA Cup Final

Slaidburn Street, SW10
April 1970

Best Forgotten
George Best of the Los Angeles
Aztecs preparing to take on the
New York Cosmos in a North
American Soccer League match.
The Aztecs lost 6–0

7th May 1976

Projection Room
The Kop, Anfield
Circa 1972

Wash And Go
Prior to their first season in
the Football League,
Wimbledon's socks soak
next to the players' toy boat

9th August 1977

Tools Of The Trade
Terry Venables' pre-match
preparations for QPR

18th November 1972

Face In The Crowd
Dave Thomas comes to
an unscheduled stop

QPR v Aston Villa
10th March 1973

Look Back In Anger

Emlyn Hughes kicks the ball away after Poland score the first of the two goals by which they beat England in a World Cup qualifier

6th June 1973

On Reflection
Ally McLeod, in contemplative
mood at Scotland's World Cup
headquarters, Córdoba, Argentina

June 1978

Lost Cause
Billy Bremner reflects on
Leeds' FA Cup Final replay
defeat against Chelsea

29th April 1970

Damaged Goods
Rodney Marsh limps off during his
League debut for Manchester City

18th March 1972

Previous page

Double Meaning
The aftermath of the 'offside' goal that helped give
West Brom their only away win of the season and
deprived Leeds of their unbeaten home record
and the 1970–71 League championship

17th April 1971

This Year's Model
Bobby Moore pondering
England's forthcoming defence
of the Jules Rimet Trophy

1970

Wing Play
A Brazilian flag-bearer a
the Mexico World Cup
opening ceremony

31st May 1970

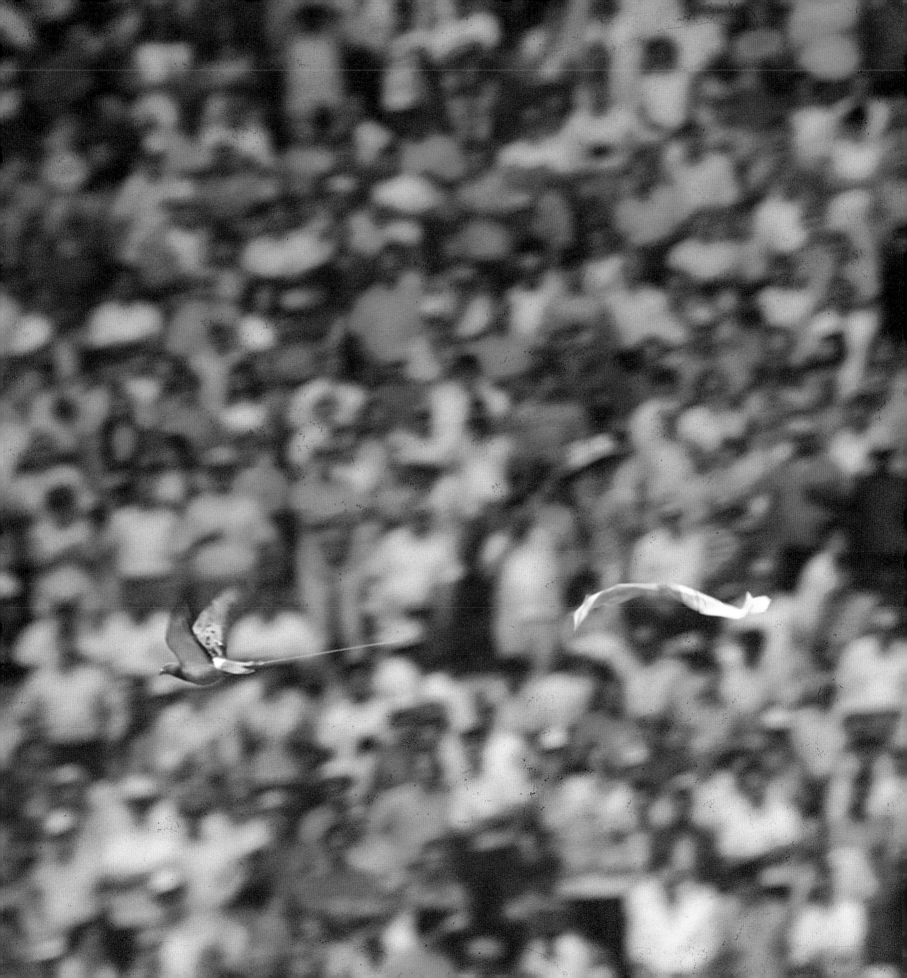

Best-Laid Plans
Sunderland manager Bob Stokoe
relaxes at Selsdon Park golf course
a few days before the FA Cup Final
victory against Leeds United

4th May 1973

Building Bridges
ec Podd, from St Kitts in the
aribbean. 494 League appearances
s a full back for Bradford City

irca 1973

City Folk
The Maine Road players and
backroom staff

1977

Dream Team
Watford have scored; chairman Elto
John celebrates; manager Graham
Taylor takes it all in his stride

October 1977

Final Thoughts
Gerd Müller leaves the pitch after West
Germany's 2–0 win over Yugoslavia in the
World Cup 2nd Round

26th June 1974

Net Result
A Gerd Müller penalty for West
Germany against Bulgaria in a
World Cup 1st Round game

7th June 1970

oll Of Honour
ary Bailey of Manchester
nited, defending his goal
om advancing toilet paper
nd West Bromwich Albion

Jth December 1978

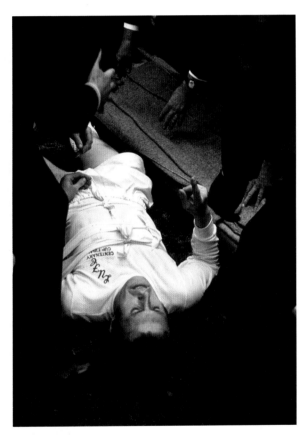

Helping Hands
Leeds United forward Mick Jones about to
be stretchered off with a dislocated elbow
during the FA Cup Final against Arsenal

6th May 1972

Military Precision
An Argentine soldier stands guard at the
newly-opened Córdoba stadium, shortly
before its inaugural match, Peru v Scotland,
in the World Cup Finals

27th May 1978

The World At His Feet
Diego Maradona appears for
Argentina in a FIFA exhibition
match against Holland

Berne, Switzerland
22nd May 1979

Flag-Bearer
An Arsenal fan before
the FA Cup Final. Terry
Neill's side overcame
Manchester United, 3–2

15th May 1979

After A Fashion
Arsenal midfielder
George Graham steps
out in beige

Circa 1970

Off The Rails
A train wrecked by Oxford fans returning from a pre-season friendly at Hereford

20th August 1973

Vantage Point
A wall overlooking the ground provides a precarious view of the FA Cup 4th Round game between Sutton United and Leeds

24th January 1970

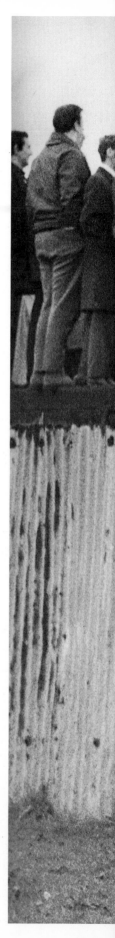

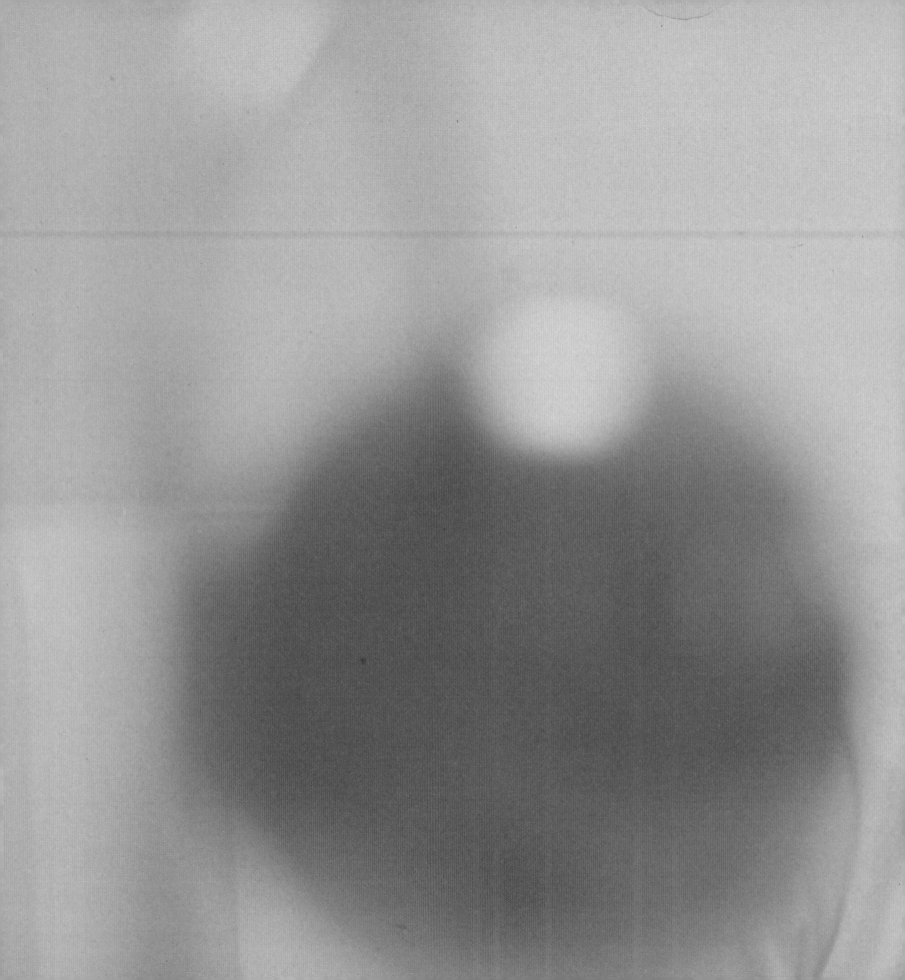

Previous page

International Call-Up
Pelé fields questions about Brazil's forthcoming defence of the World Cup

Circa 1973

Friendly Fire
Martin Buchan and Kenny Dalglish coming off the pitch after a friendly between Argentina and Scotland at the Bombonera Stadium, Buenos Aires. The game had finished 1–1; Vincente Pernia of Argentina and Willie Johnston of Scotland had been sent off

18th June 1977

The Gentile Touch
Juventus defender Claudio Gentile is sent off in extra time of a European Cup Semi-Final versus Bruges. Juventus lost 2–1 on aggregate

12th April 1978

Eye Level
Johan Cruyff scores while
guesting for the New York
Cosmos in an exhibition
match at Giants Stadium

1978

Mind Over Matter
West Germany's coach,
Helmut Schoen, just prior to
his team's unsuccessful
defence of the World Cup

1978

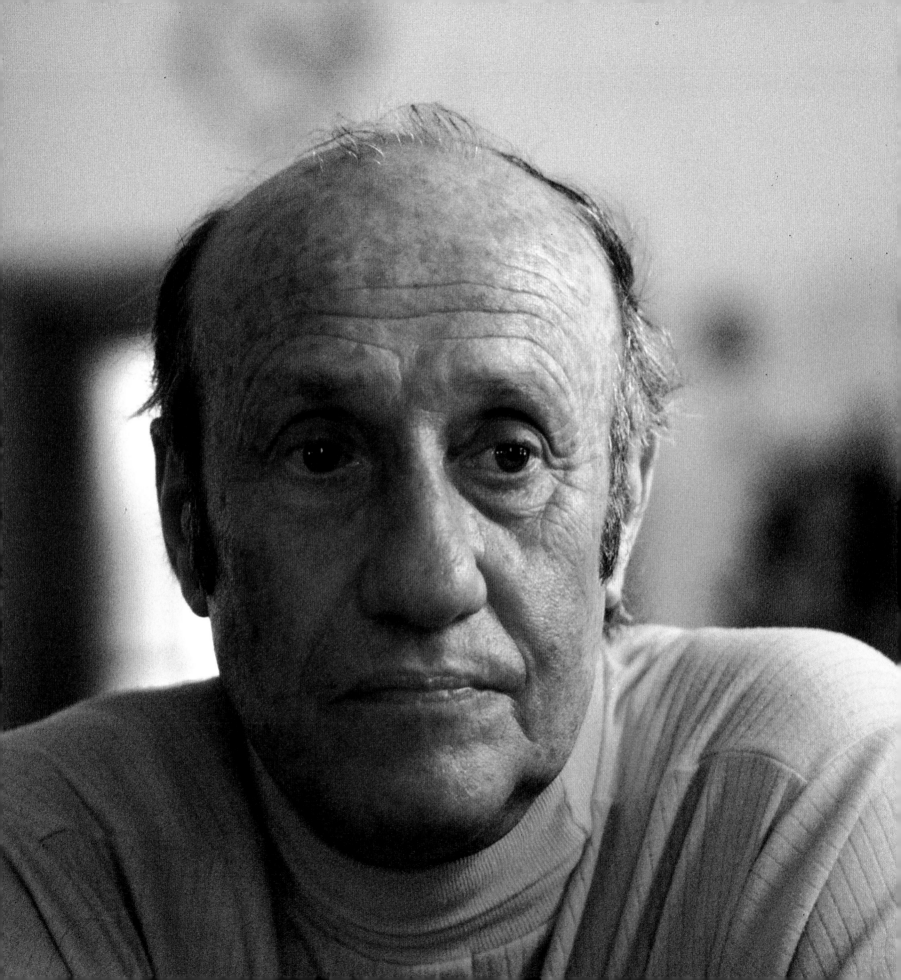

Don't Look Back
Peter Osgood training
at Southampton

Circa 1976

Eastender
Jimmy Greaves'
debut for West Ham

21st March 1970

Shadows And Fog
Czechoslovakia v England match abandoned; the officials disappear into the haze along with England's chances. They lost the re-arranged game 2–1, thereby failing to qualify for the 1976 European Championship; Czechoslovakia won the tournament

29th November 1975

Shot!

A Photographic Record of Football in the Seventies

First published in Great Britain 1994
by H. F. & G. Witherby
A Cassell imprint
Villiers House, 41/47 Strand, London WC2N 5JE

© *When Saturday Comes*
and H. F. & G. Witherby 1994
Foreword © Eamonn McCabe 1994

A catalogue record for this book is available from
the British Library

ISBN 0 85493 237 2

Printed in Great Britain
by Butler & Tanner Ltd, London and Frome.
Typeset by Fastpoint Ltd, London

Photo Credits

Front Cover:

Change Strip Mirror Syndication International

Back Cover:

Mirror Syndication International (*top*) and Colorsport (2)

Heat Of The Moment Peter Robinson

Body Language Bob Thomas/Les Williamson

Throw Back Mirror Syndication International

Dressing Down Frank Herrmann

Fair Exchange Eamonn McCabe

Goal Bound Bob Thomas/Ray Green

Matter Of Opinion Associated Press

Easily Dismissed Mirror Syndication International

Local Hero Action Images

Fever Pitch Press Association

Sign Of The Times Eamonn McCabe

Moment In Time Associated Press

Best Remembered Bob Thomas/Ray Green

Told In Confidence LWT

Pitch Inspectors Hulton Deutsch

Football Focus Frank Herrmann

Pastures New Peter Robinson

Bob And Frank Mirror Syndication International

Crowd Pleasers Mirror Syndication International

Spanish Eyes Colorsport/Andrew Cowie

Up For The Cup Peter Robinson

Down Beat Mirror Syndication International

Detroit Spinner Mirror Syndication International

Blues Brothers Peter Robinson

Cat's Eyes Eamonn McCabe

Frozen In Time Hulton Deutsch

Seconds Out Rex Features

Forward Thinking Bob Thomas/Ray Green

Cardboard City *Guardian*/Dennis Thorpe

Street Level Hulton Deutsch

Stretcher Case Mirror Syndication International

Built For Speed Hulton Deutsch

Over And Out Press Association

Centre Of Attention Bob Thomas/Ray Green

Pressure Points Popperfoto

World In Motion Associated Press

Blurred Memory Eamonn McCabe

Penalty Appeal Popperfoto

Keeping Up Appearances Mirror Syndication International

A European Place Colorsport/Andrew Cowie

Oblivious Colorsport/Mike Wall

Mirror Image Colorsport/Andrew Cowie

Smoke Signals Colorsport/Colin Elsey

Office Politics Mirror Syndication International

Striking A Pose Mirror Syndication International

After Hours Mirror Syndication International

Gimme Shelter Hulton Deutsch

Tunnel Vision Hulton Deutsch

Safe Keeping Bob Thomas/Ray Green

The Getaway Vehicle Hulton Deutsch

Derby Winner Colorsport/Mike Wall

Attention Seeker Peter Robinson

Screen Test Peter Robinson

Stretching The Point Eamonn McCabe

Suit Yourself Mirror Syndication International

Cold Remedy Peter Robinson

Mud Lark Colorsport/Mike Wall

Swapping Sides Mirror Syndication International

Blood Sport Action Images

Men At Work Frank Herrmann

In The Balance Bob Thomas/Ray Green

Billy Idol Hulton Deutsch

Final Straw Hulton Deutsch

High Numbers Mirror Syndication International

Trend Setter Mirror Syndication International

Best Forgotten Colorsport/Stewart Fraser

Chelsea Girls Hulton Deutsch

Wash And Go Hulton Deutsch

Projection Room Bob Thomas/Ray Green

Tools Of The Trade Colorsport/Stewart Fraser

Face In The Crowd Colorsport/Andrew Cowie

Look Back In Anger Mirror Syndication International

On Reflection *Glasgow Herald and Evening Post*

Lost Cause Popperfoto

Injury Time *Guardian*/Ken Giller

Damaged Goods Bob Thomas/Les Williamson

Double Meaning Press Association

This Year's Model Mirror Syndication International

Wing Play Mirror Syndication International

Building Bridges Peter Robinson

Best-Laid Plans *Guardian*

City Folk Bob Thomas/Les Williamson

Dream Team Keith Dobney

Final Thoughts Peter Robinson

Net Result Associated Press

Roll Of Honour Mirror Syndication International

Helping Hands Bob Thomas/Ray Green

Military Precision Associated Press

The World At His Feet Popperfoto

Flag-Bearer Hulton Deutsch

After A Fashion Action Images

Off The Rails Hulton Deutsch

Vantage Point Hulton Deutsch

International Call-Up Colorsport

The Gentile Touch Bob Thomas/Bob Thomas

Friendly Fire Peter Robinson

Eye Level Peter Robinson

Mind Over Matter Eamonn McCabe

Don't Look Back Eamonn McCabe

Saints And Sinners Eamonn McCabe

Eastender Bob Thomas/Ray Green

Shadows And Fog Colorsport/Andrew Cowie

The copyright is held by the first named; where this is a company, the photographer is also credited if known

Thanks to: Eamonn McCabe, Peter Robinson, Andrew Cowie at Colorsport, Dave Samuels at Mirror Syndication International, Caroline Theakstone at Hulton Deutsch, Monte Fresco at Bob Thomas, Frank Herrmann, Philip Cornwall, Jamie Rainbow, Tim Bradford, Tony Ageh, Ian Preece at Gollancz, Joan Fisher at Associated Press, Tony Murray at *Glasgow Herald*, Lance Bellers, Matthew Smith, Jonathan Westbrook, Steve Hale, Empics, Anne-Marie Cobbe, and Tim Maddox at Fastpoint for their help with this book

Shot! was edited, compiled and published in association with *When Saturday Comes*, 4th Floor, 2 Pear Tree Court, London EC1R 0DS